Pressure C

Wonderfully Delicious A̱   *...ipes For Fast*
And Easy Meals

Sara Banks

Symbol LLC

PRESSURE COOKER RECIPES

Introduction

I want to thank you and congratulate you for purchasing "Pressure Cooker Recipes-Wonderfully Delicious And Simple Recipes For Fast And Easy Meals." If you love to use your pressure cooker you no doubt appreciate its ability to save you tons of time on a daily or weekly basis. Many people I know struggle to keep things fresh and interesting when cooking with a pressure cooker. Because of that I have put together my top recipes to use that I know you and your family will just love.

They are not only delicious but also simple to make which is what we are all after in the end.

Let's get started!

Thank-you

Sara Banks

The Magic Of Pressure Cooking

Most of us wish to make home cooked meals so that we live a healthy and fulfilling life but the only problem is the fact that cooking normally takes lots of time. Most of us don't have that time in our hands; that's why we end up turning to fast foods and other unhealthy foods. This doesn't have to be the case since you can start preparing all your meals fast and easy using a pressure cooker. Actually, food that could take hours of cooking will probably only take minutes on the pressure cooker allowing you to save lots of time, which you can then direct towards doing other important tasks. I have compiled tons of great recipes that you can try at home for breakfast, lunch, dinner, dessert, salads, soups and stews just to mention a few.

Breakfast Recipes

Breakfast Risotto

Makes 3 servings

Ingredients

1 ½ cups Arborio rice

2 tablespoons butter

1 ½ teaspoons cinnamon

2 apples, cored and diced

1 cup apple juice

1/3 cup brown sugar

¼ teaspoon salt

½ cup dried cherries

3 cups 1% milk

Instructions

Heat the butter in pressure cooker for around two minutes then add the rice and cook for 3-4 minutes while stirring constantly until the rice becomes opaque.

Add the spices, brown sugar and apples. Add in the milk and juice and stir. Cover the pressure cooker, select high pressure and cook for six minutes. After the six minutes turn off the cooker and use quick pressure release. Remove the pressure cooker lid carefully and add in the dried cherries then stir.

Serve this topped with sliced almonds and milk.

Hard-Boiled Eggs

Makes 8 eggs

Ingredients

4 cups ice cubes

4 cups of cold water

8 fresh eggs

2 cups water or more

Instructions

Fill the pressure cooker with water as specified by the manufacturer then insert the eggs into the steamer basket and place it above the water then completely secure the lid and set the pressure to low.

Cook the eggs for 6 minutes while maintaining low pressure then remove the cooker from heat and allow pressure to be released in about 5 minutes.

In a large bowl, mix ice with cold water and use the quick-release method to open the cooker. Using an oven mitt or spoon, transfer the hot eggs to the ice water and allow cooling for 30 minutes.

Oatmeal Apple Crisp

Makes 2 servings

Ingredients

2 ½ cups water

1/3 cup melted margarine

½ teaspoon salt

1 teaspoon cinnamon

½ cup brown sugar

1/3 cup flour

1 cup quick cooking oats

1 tablespoon lemon juice

4 cups apples, peeled and sliced

Instructions

Sprinkle the lemon juice on the apples and then combine oats, salt, margarine, brown sugar, flour and cinnamon.

Arrange alternating layers of the oat and apple mixture that begin and end with apples inside a buttered metallic bowl that will fit in a pressure cooker then cover the bowl using aluminum foil.

Into the pressure cooker, place water and position the metallic bowl on a rack inside the cooker before securing the lid then place the pressure regulator on a vent pipe and then cook for about 20 minutes while the pressure regulator rocks slowly; cool and serve.

Pressure Cooker Breakfast Hash

Makes 4-6 servings

Ingredients

6 small potatoes shredded

1 cup of crumbled bacon, sausage or ham

1 cup of grated cheese

6 eggs, beaten

Instructions

Coat the pressure cooker with cooking oil then preheat it without the lid. Shred the potatoes in the processor then squeeze the moisture out and then brown in the preheated pressure cooker.

Beat the eggs and set them aside then break up the potatoes and add about ¼ cup of water followed by the remaining ingredients then mix them gently.

Seal the lid before bringing it to pressure and then serve the hash with toast immediately once it is well cooked.

Lentils with Chorizo Sausage

Makes 2 servings

Ingredients

Salt

1 bay leaf

½ teaspoon paprika

¾ liter cold water

4 garlic cloves

1 medium onion

1 large carrot

100g chorizo sausage

225g brown lentils

Instructions

In the pressure cooker, put lentils, onion, peeled carrot, garlic cloves and add whole vegetables and bay leaves.

Chop the chorizo to about 4 pieces and put in the cooker, followed by cold water, paprika and salt to taste. Boil the contents while the cooker is uncovered.

Place the lid after the contents start to boil and seal, allowing cooking for about 8 minutes. Remove from heat and allow the pressure to disappear naturally then discard the bay leaves.

Blend carrots, garlic and onions until smooth then return the vegetable puree t the lentils then mix well.

Pressure Cooked Sandwich

Makes 1 serving

Ingredients

1 thin slice of prosciutto

1 cup water

1 egg

¼ teaspoon olive oil

2 slices rye bread

1 tablespoon shredded cheddar cheese

Instructions

Add the water to the pressure cooker then put in a streamer tray. Grease the bottom of your rameskin with the olive oil and place the prosciutto at the bottom of the rameskin. Add the egg and season with black pepper if need be then sprinkle the shredded cheese at the top.

Cover the rameskin with tin foil, put in the steam basket and set the basket in the pressure cooker right on top of the trivet. Close the pressure cooker and heat to high.

Immediately it reaches the low pressure point, start timing for six minutes. After the six minutes, allow the pressure cooker to cool.

Meanwhile, toast your slices of bread. Open the pressure cooker lid carefully and remove the rameskin. Run a butter knife round the edge of egg then tip it out to the slices of rye.

Serve immediately.

New England Clam chowder

Makes 2 servings

Ingredients

¼ cup butter

1 quart light cream

2 cans (8-ounce) minced clams

2 cups water

1/8 teaspoon pepper

2 teaspoons salt

4 cups cubed potatoes

2 cups chopped onions

4 slices bacon, chopped

Instructions

In a pressure cooker, sauté onions and bacon over medium low heat and add pepper, water, potatoes and salt then seal the cover completely and place the pressure regulator on the vent pipe and then cook for about 5 minutes at about 15 pounds pressure. Let the pressure come down on its own then drain the clams.

Add the clams slowly followed by butter, cream and 1 cup clam liquid, stirring thoroughly then simmer for about 10 minutes in an open pressure cooker.

White Beans with Tuscan Lamb Shanks

Makes 4 servings

Ingredients

3 ½ cups water

1 cup navy beans, dried and picked over

2 rosemary sprigs

1 (14-ounces) can diced tomatoes in juice

3 garlic cloves, thinly sliced

2 celery ribs, chopped

2 medium carrots, chopped

1 large onion, chopped

2 tablespoons olive oil

For the garnish: chopped flat-leaf parsley and extra-virgin olive oil for drizzling

2 lamb shanks (2 pounds total)

Directions

Dry the lamb shanks and season with ¼ teaspoon pepper and ½ teaspoon salt. In a pressure cooker, heat the oil in medium heat until it shimmers before browning shanks one at a time then transfer the lamb shanks to a plate.

Add celery, onions, garlic and carrots to the cooker and sauté to golden brown for 6 minutes. Add the rosemary and tomato with juice and cook for a minute, while stirring then stir in ¼ teaspoon of pepper, the beans, ½ teaspoon of salt and then add water.

Return the lamb shanks to the pressure cooker and boil for 30 minutes, ensuring the lid is sealed. To cool the cooker, run cold water over the lid without removing the lid until pressure decreases then remove the lid, discard the rosemary, then transfer the shanks to a cutting board, and then coarsely shred the meat before spooning over the vegetable mixture and beans into large bowls, and top with the lamb shanks and sauce.

Soups

Italian Chicken Soup

Makes 8 servings

Ingredients

1 cup mild salsa

1 bag (16 ounce) chopped fresh spinach leaves, chopped

15 ounce (1 can) chickpeas (garbanzo beans) drained

3 cups chicken stock

½ cup of fresh parsley, chopped

1 bone-in chicken breast half with skin removed

1 cup green lentils

½ cup pearl barley

3 cloves garlic, minced

4 Italian turkey sausage links, casings

2 teaspoons olive oil

1 sliced medium onion, diced

Instructions

In a pressure cooker, heat 1 teaspoon of olive oil over medium heat and then add sausage meat and cook until it turns brown, and break it into crumbles. Transfer the sausage to a plate and drain the oil, then add 1 teaspoon olive oil to the pressure cooker and cook the onion and garlic until the onion turns transparent then add barley and stir for a minute.

Place the sausage back to the pressure cooker and add parsley, chicken stock, lentils and chicken to the pressure cooker ensuring to add enough stock to cover the chicken completely.

Close the cover and place the pressure regulator on the vent pipe and then put the cooker into full pressure in high heat for 15 minutes and reduce heat for 9 minutes to medium high ensuring that the pressure regulator remains in a slow and constant rocking motion; adjust the heat if necessary.

Remove the cooker from heat and allow it to cool. Open the pressure cooker and remove the chicken, shred the meat and return it to the soup. Before serving, add salsa, spinach and garbanzo beans, and stir to blend as you heat through.

Split Pea and Ham Soup

Makes 6-8 servings

Ingredients

Sherry wine (optional)

1 ½ teaspoons dried thyme

2 celery ribs, diced

2 carrots, diced

1 onion, diced

1 small ham bone or 1 pound ham, chunks

8 cups water

1 pound of dried split peas

Instructions

Place all the ingredients except the sherry wine in a pressure cooker and half fill the cooker with water.

Seal the cooker and place the rocker on vent pipe, before bringing the contents to high-heat pressure, and time for about 20 minutes. Allow the pressure to remove its steam on its own. If you are using pork bone, remove it from the pressure cooker and pull its meat off before adding to soup.

Season with salt and serve with sherry splash if required.

Yogurt and Barley Soup

Makes 6 servings

Ingredients:

Salt and freshly ground pepper

2 ½ tablespoons of chopped fresh mint

720 ml plain yogurt, lightly beaten

1.2 liters of chicken stock

3 tablespoons of pearl barley, rinsed

110g of finely chopped onion

1 ½ tablespoon of butter

Instructions

Heat the butter in the pressure cooker and sauté the onion until it has wilted, before adding the stock and barley.

Close the lid before bringing the cooker to pressure then lower the heat and cook on high pressure for about 15 minutes. Release the pressure using the natural method and allow the contents to cool while the cooker is open.

You can transfer to another container and then chill it in the refrigerator. Later, stir the yogurt and add 1 ½ tablespoons of mint, before seasoning it with pepper and salt to taste. Garnish with the remaining mint and serve it when cold.

Rapid Chicken Stock

Makes 8 servings

Ingredients

1 teaspoon sea salt

4 quarts cold water

15 whole black peppercorns

10 cloves garlic

1 leftover chicken carcass

1 large carrot, cut into 4 pieces

1 large onion, quartered

1 stalk celery, quartered (optional)

Instructions

Place the peppercorns, garlic cloves, chicken carcass, celery, carrot and onion into a pressure cooker then add water to two-third fullness, and then secure the lid.

Heat the cooker to maximum pressure over high heat then reduce heat to medium low and then cook for 30 minutes under the maximum pressure. After half an hour, remove the pot from heat and let the pressure be released naturally.

Remove the lid then strain the stock into a different bowl and discard the vegetables and chicken bones. Let the mixture cool at room temperature before transferring to the fridge. Cooling makes the fat to rise to the surface and solidify; you can then skim the fat off completely then season with sea salt.

Main Dishes

Asian Pepper Steak

Makes 6 servings

Ingredients

Basmati rice, cooked

2 tablespoons potato starch or cornstarch

2 tablespoons water

¼ cup soy sauce

4 green onions, coarsely chopped

1 green bell pepper, sliced

2 tomatoes cut into eighths

½ teaspoon red pepper flakes

1 teaspoon ginger root, grated

½ teaspoon salt

1 teaspoon light brown sugar

1 tablespoon sherry

½ cup beef broth

1 pound beef round steak, cut into -3 x 1/2

2 cloves garlic, sliced

1 large onion, sliced

2 tablespoons olive oil

1 tablespoon sesame oil

Instructions

Heat the oils in a pressure cooker and add garlic and onion and sauté for about 2 minutes then add the beef strips while continuously stirring and cook the content for 1 minute in high heat.

Stir in the pepper flakes, ginger root, salt, brown sugar, sherry and the broth and secure the lid. Bring the pressure cooker to maximum pressure by heating to high heat then lower the heat to low and cook for 10 minutes in high pressure ensuring that you maintain the pressure at maximum. Allow the cooker to release pressure in accordance to the manufacturer's instructions then remove the lid.

Stir in the green onions, tomatoes and bell pepper and secure the lid again before heating the cooker until it attains medium high pressure then lower the heat to low and maintain pressure then cook for 2 minutes. Allow the cooker to release pressure according to the directions of the manufacturer then remove the lid.

Mix potato starch, water and sauce in a small bowl and then mix until you obtain a smooth consistency. Add in the veggies and the beef gradually while stirring gently until creamy and thickened then serve the beef and veggies over the rice.

Chuck Roast Dish

Makes 6 servings

Ingredients

14.5 ounce (1 can) beef broth

1.2 ounce (1 can) package brown gravy mix

1 ounce package dry ranch style dressing mix

1 ounce package Italian salad dressing mix

1 large onion, sliced

3 pounds beef chuck roast

2 tablespoons oil

Instructions

In pressure cooker, heat oil in medium heat ensuring the lid is open, browning the roast through the sides of hot coil.

Mix the gravy mix, Italian salad dressing mix and ranch dressing mix in a bowl or cup. The dressings should be well sprinkled over the brown roast, before you pour the beef broth followed by chopped onion.

Put the lid and lock the pressure cooker and let the mixture cook in high heat to build pressure, up to when the indicator of the cooker sounds. Reduce the heat to medium and continue cooking for about 45 minutes. Disconnect the pressure cooker and remove from heat, allowing cooling for 5 minutes.

To help release pressure, run cool water over it and then unseal the lid. You may use the juices as its own juice or thicken using cornstarch or flour and have a delicious gravy.

Chicken with Duck Sauce

Makes 6 servings

Ingredients

¼ cup chicken broth

¼ cup wine

½ teaspoon dried marjoram

½ teaspoon paprika

Salt and pepper to taste

1 (3 pound) whole chicken, cut into small pieces

1 tablespoon olive oil

Duck Sauce:

2 tablespoons of honey

1 ½ teaspoons minced fresh ginger root

2 tablespoons white vinegar

¼ cup apricot preserves

Instructions

Preheat pressure cooker then add in the olive oil and heat over medium-high heat ensuring to keep the lid off. Add in the chicken then brown it all the sides and then remove it from the cooker then season the chicken with marjoram, salt, pepper and paprika, before draining and discarding the fat from the cooker. Mix in chicken broth and wine, and scrap any bits of food stuck to the bottom of the pressure cooker.

Heat the chicken again in medium-high heat, seal the pressure cooker and raise the pressure to high then heat for 8 minutes, to make the chicken tender. Lower the pressure before removing the lid, but maintain the internal temperature at 82 degrees Celsius or (180 degrees F)

Take out the chicken from the pressure cooker then place it on a serving dish and add vinegar, honey, apricot leaves and ginger. Boil and cook the mixture while uncovered up until a thick syrupy substance has been formed, approximately in 10 minutes. To serve, spoon the mixture over the chicken.

Easy Pressure Cooker Pot Roast

Makes 8 servings

Ingredients

4 large potatoes, peeled and cut into bite-size pieces

4 carrots, peeled and cut into bite-size pieces

1 large onion, cut into 4 wedges

1 ½ tablespoons Worcestershire sauce

1 (14.5 ounce) can beef broth

1 pinch onion powder

1 pinch seasoned salt

Ground black pepper to taste

1 (3 pound) boneless beef chuck roast, trimmed

2 tablespoons vegetable oil

Instructions

Preheat the pressure cooker then add in the oil and then heat over medium-high heat then brown all the sides of the beef roast in the hot oil and season with salt, onion powder and pepper.

Pour in the Worcestershire sauce and the beef broth, followed by quartered onion then cover the cooker. Heat the cooker to maximum pressure, then reduce the heat to low and cook for half an hour ensuring to maintain full pressure.

To lower the cooker's pressure, follow the quick release method then mix in potatoes and the carrots and cover the cooker before returning the cooker to heat. Heat the cooker to maximum pressure then cook for 15 more minutes and then lower the cooker's pressure using quick release method before transferring the vegetables and the roast to a dish for serving.

Pressure Cooker Pot Roast

Makes 6 servings

Ingredients

½ cup cold water

3 onions, peeled

8 potatoes, peeled and halved

2 ½ cups of cold water

2 (1 ounce) packages of dry onion soup mix

¼ cup of vegetable shortening

1/3 cup all-purpose flour

Salt and ground black pepper

3 pounds beef rump roast

Instructions

Start by seasoning the rump roast with pepper and salt every side then coat it with flour ensuring to reserve some flour for the gravy.

In a pressure cooker, melt the vegetable shortening over medium-high heat then brown all sides of the rump roast in the hot seasoning and then sprinkle the onion soup mix on the rump roast and pour in about 2 cups of water or more depending on what your pressure cooker demands.

Close the cover of the cooker then heat to full pressure on high heat, then reduce the heat to low then cook for 90-120 minutes ensuring that you maintain the pressure cooker at full pressure.

To verify if the cooking is done, release the pressure completely before opening the cover to check if the meat is fork tender. If tender, add onions and potatoes ensuring the vegetables are inside the cooking liquid (You can rearrange the roast in the water so that the veggies can fit or add some more water if you have to). Cover the lid completely and bring the cooker to full pressure. Lower the heat to low while ensuring that the pressure cooker remains at full pressure then cook for 10 minutes under low heat before releasing the pressure and transferring the vegetables and meat to a serving board.

To make the gravy

Boil the cooking liquid then whisk any reserved flour into ½ cup of cold water. Into the boiling broth, whisk the flour mixture until the mixture has thickened enough, ensuring to stir after every 3 minutes then serve the gravy with vegetables and pot roast.

Authentic Beef Curry

Makes 6 servings

Ingredients

1 teaspoon ginger paste

2 pounds beef chuck (boneless) cut into 1 ½ -inch pieces

1 teaspoon garlic powder

1 cup water

1 teaspoon cayenne pepper

5 finely sliced green Chile peppers

1 onion, chopped

1 teaspoon turmeric

1 teaspoon ground coriander

1 teaspoon ground cumin

1 ½ inch cinnamon sticks

2 whole cloves

3 whole cardamom seeds

3 tablespoons olive oil

6 cloves garlic, minced

Instructions

In a pressure cooker, heat olive oil over medium heat and add onion then stir well until the onion has softened and turned translucent for about 5 minutes. Lower the heat to medium low then cook the onion for additional 15-20 minutes under medium low heat until the onion becomes dark brown and very tender ensuring to stir continuously.

Add in the cinnamon sticks, cloves, cardamom seeds, ginger paste, green chiles and garlic and cook while stirring until the garlic starts turning brown- this will take about 3-5 more minutes. Add in the water, cayenne pepper, garlic powder, turmeric, coriander and cumin and simmer until almost all the water has evaporated and the mixture has thickened.

Add the beef to the pressure cooker then seal the lid and bring the cooker to high pressure and cook until the beef is tender; for about 40 minutes then allow the pressure to release naturally after cooking then serve.

Pressure Cooker Pork Tenderloin

Makes 6 servings

Ingredients

¼ cup lemon juice

¾ cup chicken broth

1 pound pork tenderloin

¼ teaspoon salt

½ teaspoon red pepper flakes

2 cloves garlic, sliced

¼ cup lime juice

¼ cup olive oil

¼ cup fresh cilantro leaves

Instructions

In a blender, blend the red pepper flakes, garlic, lime juice, olive oil, cilantro and salt until smooth and transfer to a big resealable plastic bag. Add pork tenderloin to the plastic bag then shake well to cover the tenderloin with the marinade. Remove any air from the bag before sealing then to refrigerate overnight for 8 hours.

In the bottom of a pressure cooker, stir lemon juice and chicken broth together and lay the tenderloin into the pressure cooker ensuring it is submerged in the liquid. Pour any remaining marinade over the tenderloin.

Secure the cooker and cook under high heat until you attain maximum pressure then lower the heat to medium and cook for about 25 minutes and then remove the mixture from heat and let it cool for about 5 minutes. To help release the accumulated pressure from the cooker, run cold water and then uncover the lid. You can slice the tenderloin into medallions when serving.

Desserts

Vanilla Spice Poached Plums

Makes 3 cups

Ingredients

1 ½ cups Water

2 tablespoons Honey

3 Cardamom pods

4 Cloves

2 Cinnamon sticks

1 Star anise

1 Vanilla bean pod, split and seeded

1 ½ pounds Fresh plums (15 small ones)

Instructions

Cut the plums into 2 halves, remove the pit and put the contents into the bottom of the pressure cooker then split the vanilla bean into two halves lengthwise and scrape the seeds out of each half using a knife.

To the pressure cooker, add sufficient water, the honey, spices and the vanilla pod halves and seal the pot. Heat the pressure cooker to high heat to bring the pressure to maximum then lower the heat to medium then cook the contents in medium-heat for 15 minutes while the pressure is at its maximum. Turn off the heat and allow the pressure to release naturally then remove the lid, and remove the plums and then half the remaining liquid by heating on high heat.

You can then store the plums with the liquid in a glass jar (airtight) then place in the fridge or serve the mixture over pudding, applesauce, yogurt or cake.

Hazelnut Flan

Makes 8

Ingredients

For the Custard:

2 tablespoons Hazelnut syrup

½ cup whipping cream

1 teaspoon vanilla extract

2 cups whole milk

Pinch of salt

1/3 cup granulated sugar

2 egg yolks

3 whole eggs

For the Caramel:

¼ cup water

¾ cup granulated sugar

Instructions

How to prepare the caramel

Add ¼ cup water and ¾ cup sugar in a medium saucepan then boil the contents, cover the pan and then let it boil for about 2 minutes or until the sugar crystals are fully dissolved.

Take off the lid and cook while uncovered until amber, but do not stir. Instead, swirl the pan gently to ensure that you keep the mixture moving. Ensure that it doesn't get too dark otherwise it will burn. Pour the mixture into 8 (6 ounces) ungreased custard cups ensuring to tilt the bottom completely then set these aside.

Whisk the eggs and yolks in a large bowl then mix with 1/3 cup of sugar plus some salt. Heat milk in a sauce pan until it starts bubbling on medium heat. Add the hot milk gradually to the eggs to temper them, before whisking in hazelnut syrup, cream and vanilla then strain into a measuring bowl that has a pitcher or pour sprout.

Measure 1½ cups water, add to the cooker placing the trivet at the bottom and then pour in the custard into custard cup lined with caramel and cover with foil before placing on trivet in the cooker then create a second layer by stacking the cups.

Lock the cooker's lid and cook for 6 minutes under high pressure. Turn off the pressure cooker and allow the pressure to drop naturally for 10 minutes then perform a quick release to get rid of any remaining pressure after which you can remove the lid. Perform a quick release for accumulated pressure until the valve drops when you remove the lid.

Remove the cups carefully and place them on a wire rack to cool while uncovered. Once they have cooled, refrigerate them while covered using a plastic wrap for about 4 hours or overnight.

Run a very thin knife around the outer side of the ramekins then hold a plate on top and then flip everything over. You can serve when topped with chopped hazelnuts and whipped cream.

Ham Hocks and Beans

Makes 8 servings

Ingredients

Salt

1 teaspoon pepper

1 tablespoon oregano

1 large bay leaf

6 cloves garlic, minced

1 large onion, chopped

4-6 ham hocks

1 bag dry beans

Instructions

Prepare the beans by removing any gravel before washing then place the onions, garlic, beans and ham rock in a pressure cooker and then fill with water.

Add the spices and then cover the pressure cooker and heat until the pressure cooker attains maximum pressure, lower the temperature to medium and cook for about 10 minutes ensuring that the pressure is at its maximum. Turn off the heat and use the quick release method to get rid of the pressure. Extract the meat from the hams and return them to the soup then discard the fat and bones.

Collard Greens

Makes 4 servings

Ingredients

1 teaspoon sugar

½ teaspoon salt

1 tablespoon balsamic vinegar

3 minced garlic cloves

1 small onion, sliced thinly

2 tablespoons diced tomatoes /2 tablespoons tomato puree

2 tablespoons olive oil

½ cup chicken broth

1 bunch fresh collard greens

Instructions

Soak the collard greens for about 30 minutes in a sink filled with water to remove dirt.

Mix the tomato puree, garlic, chicken broth, vinegar, oil and onion in a pressure cooker and then stir thoroughly to combine all the ingredients then remove the soaked greens from the water one by one ensuring that you don't disturb the water to keep dirt at the bottom while the greens float. Chop the thick stems that are at the base of the greens then chop the remaining parts into small pieces and stack them on top of each other then roll into cigar shaped bundles and then cut the greens into 1-2 inch wide pieces.

Mix the stems and the greens with salt and sugar and then add them to the pot then toss well to coat with the oil mixture. Cook in the pressure cooker for 20 minutes

Pressure Cooker Banana Pudding

Makes 4 servings

Ingredients

2 cups water

½ teaspoon pure vanilla extract

1 ½ teaspoons dark rum

¼ cup sour cream

¼ cup sweetened condensed milk

½ cup half-and-half

3 tablespoons sugar

2 large egg yolks

1 medium ripe banana

Instructions

Get 6 ounces soufflé dishes at hand then puree the ripe banana in a blender or food processor.

Mix the condensed milk, rum, eggs, half-and-half, vanilla and sour cream and ensure to mix well then strain the mix through a fine strainer.

Transfer the mixture to soufflé dishes and cover the contents lightly using aluminum foil, and then add 2 cups of water to the cooker. Insert the steamer basket into the pressure cooker then add the soufflé dishes ensuring that the water cannot reach the steamer. You can add trivet to keep the dishes water free and then seal the cooker and raise the pressure. To stabilize the cooker, lower the heat, allow cooking for 12 minutes then immediately release the pressure and then remove the dishes.

Remove the lid immediately and refrigerate to cool while still uncovered until the pudding becomes lukewarm. Refrigerate while covered for 2 days.

Sauces & Salads

Potato Salad

Makes 6 servings

Ingredients

1 teaspoon cider vinegar

1 teaspoon yellow mustard

½ cup mayonnaise

1 tablespoon chopped fresh dill

3 hard-cooked eggs, chopped

Salt and pepper to taste

1 stalk celery, chopped

¼ cup chopped onion

1 cup water

6 medium red potatoes, scrubbed

Instructions

Place the potatoes in a pressure cooker containing water then cook for about 3-4 minutes in high pressure. Allow the steam to be released for 3 minutes before releasing the pressure and opening the cooker. When potatoes are cool enough, peel and dice them.

Into a large bowl, alternate layers of onion, celery and potatoes and season each layer with pepper and salt and then add chopped eggs to top up and sprinkle with dill.

Mix the mustard, cider vinegar and mayonnaise in a bowl before folding the mayonnaise mixture gently into the potatoes then chill for about an hour before serving the salad.

Chili salad

Makes 6 servings

Ingredients

2 cups water

¼ teaspoon crushed red pepper flakes

½ teaspoon kosher salt, or to taste

2 teaspoons ground cumin

2 tablespoons chili powder

2 teaspoons unsweetened cocoa powder

1 tablespoon dark brown sugar

3 tablespoons tomato paste

2 (14.5 ounce) cans diced tomatoes, un-drained

2 (14.5 ounce) cans dark red kidney Beans, drained and rinsed

2 cloves garlic, minced

1 jalapeno pepper, seeded and finely chopped

1 small green bell pepper, finely chopped

1 sweet onion, chopped

2 teaspoons olive oil

1 pound ground beef

Instructions

Place the ground beef in the pressure cook then cook over medium heat until it turns crumbly and brown. After 8-10 minutes, take out the ground beef and drain off any excess fats.

Return the open pressure cooker to heat then pour in olive oil into the cooker heated to medium heat then stir the green pepper, jalapeno pepper and onion and then cook while stirring for 3-4 minutes or until the onion turns translucent then add garlic and cook while stirring for 30 more seconds. Put back the meat in the cooker, and mix with diced tomatoes, brown sugar, kidney beans, chili powder, salt, red pepper flakes, tomato paste, water, cumin, and cocoa powder.

Close the lid and bring the pressure cooker high heat then reduce the heat in order to maintain high pressure, and cook for about 8 minutes at maximum pressure. Allow 5 to 10 minutes for pressure to decrease naturally after removing the cooker from heat. Stir in the chili after pressure is released and then serve.

Pressure Cooker Apple Sauce

Makes 2 ½ cups

Ingredients

4-inch strip lemon zest

1/8 teaspoon of ground cinnamon

½ cup of sugar

½ cup of water

6 medium apples, peeled, cored and cut into ¼ inch thick wedges

Instructions

Mix together lemon zest, cinnamon, sugar, water and the apples in the pressure cooker and secure the lid, then bring it to high pressure over high-heat.

Remove the cooker from heat then quick release the pressure and then open the lid ensuring to tilt it away to block all escaping steam. Get rid of the lemon zest then stir the mixture well to break the apples into small pieces then return the cooker to heat and then cook until the applesauce is nice and thick.

Spaghetti Sauce

Makes 6 cups

Ingredients

6 cups hot cooked spaghetti or fettuccine

6-ounce Can tomato paste

28-ounce can stewed tomatoes

2 bay leaves

¼ teaspoon crushed red pepper

1 teaspoon dried oregano, crushed

1 teaspoon sugar

1/3 cup snipped fresh parsley

2 cloves garlic, minced

½ cup sliced celery (1 rib)

½ cup chopped onion (1 medium)

2 cups sliced fresh mushrooms (6 ounces)

½ pound bulk pork sausage or Italian sausage

½ pound ground beef

Instructions

Cook the sausage or beef in a pressure cooker until brown and then remove the meat, drain the fat and return it to cooker and then add tomato paste, stewed tomatoes, bay leaves, crushed red pepper, oregano, sugar, parsley, garlic, celery, onion, and the mushrooms. Seal the pressure cooker and ensure the pressure regulator is on the vent pipe.

Heat the cooker over high heat to bring the pressure to maximum then lower the heat and then cook for 10 minutes while the regulator rocks gently. Use the quick release method to release the pressure then remove the lid carefully. Remove the bay leaves and serve the sauce over spaghetti.

German Potato Salad

Makes 4 servings

Ingredients

½ teaspoon (2 ml) celery seeds

Salt and pepper to taste

1 medium onion, thinly sliced

4 medium-large potatoes in 1/4" (5 mm) slices

1 teaspoon mustard

3 tablespoons vinegar

4 teaspoons sugar

4 slices bacon

Instructions

In a pressure cooker, fry the bacon until it is crisp then remove from the cooker and drain on paper towels then reserve 1 teaspoon of the drippings then wipe the cooker well.

Mix the reserved bacon drippings, mustard, vinegar and sugar in a small bowl and pour about 1 ¾ cups water into the cooker. Arrange the onions and potatoes in layers inside a pressure cooker basket and ensure to sprinkle each layer with the reserved crumbled bacon, vinegar-mustard mixture, celery seed, pepper and salt. Lower the basket into the pressure cooker then cover the lid and bring the cooker to high pressure by heating on high heat then reduce the heat to low and cook for 2 minutes.

Allow the cooker to release the pressure through the quick release method then uncover the cooker and remove the cooker basket before serving.

Red Cabbage Salad

Makes 4 servings

Ingredients

Salt and pepper, to taste

½ teaspoon brown sugar

1-2 teaspoons red wine vinegar

1 tablespoon canola oil

¼ cup onion, chopped

2 cups red cabbage, shredded

Instructions

In a steamer basket, place red cabbage and lower it into the pressure cooker. Seal the lid and bring the pressure cooker to maximum pressure then lower the heat and cook for 2 minutes. Allow the pressure to be released automatically or through quick release method then remove the lid.

Get the steamer basket out and cool by running cold water over the red cabbage before transferring the cabbage into another bowl to add the other ingredients and then toss the contents, season with some more vinegar and serve.

Tomato Pasta Sauce

Makes 4 servings

Ingredients

½ cup water

¼ cup dry red or white wine

1 or 2 bay leaves

1 teaspoon dried parsley

2 teaspoons dried oregano

3 teaspoons dried basil

Salt and freshly ground pepper, to taste

¼ cup tomato paste

1 large can (28 fl oz) crushed canned tomatoes

2 garlic cloves, minced

¾ cup celery, finely chopped

¾ cup carrot, finely chopped

½ cup onion, finely chopped

3 tablespoons canola oil

Instructions

In the pressure cooker, heat the oil and then sauté the celery, garlic, carrot and the onion until they become soft then add the other ingredients and cover the cooker with its lid then bring the cooker to pressure by heating to high heat and lower heat. Cook for 10 minutes and allow the pressure to drop using the quick release method after which you can remove the lid. You can reduce the quantity of the sauce if it is not in its required thickness.

Stews

Basic Sabbath Stew

Makes 6-8 cups

Ingredients

1 teaspoon black pepper, freshly ground

2 teaspoons salt

6 cups of cold water

2 tablespoons oil

2 cloves garlic, finely chopped

1 onion, chopped finely

5 beef marrow or neck bones

1 ½ pound brisket, cut into large chunks

6 small red potatoes

½ cup red kidney beans

½ cup small white lima beans

½ cup medium barley

Instructions

Brown the onions and meat in a pressure cooker.

Under a running stream of cold water, rinse the barley in a sieve until it clears, and then rinse the beans well too. Peel the potatoes and then cut them into round pieces.

Add the garlic, bones, potatoes and beans into the beef onion mixture then add enough water to cover then cover the pressure cooker with the lid. Bring the cooker to maximum pressure and then reduce the heat to low and allow the mixture to cook for 45 minutes while ensuring that the cooker is at the maximum pressure. Use the quick release method to release pressure from the cooker then remove the lid. Skim any froth that might be rising to the surface.

Return the cooker to heat while uncovered and cook under low heat until done then serve.

Ratatouille Vegetable Stew

Makes 6 servings

Ingredients

¼ cup (60 ml) chicken or vegetable stock

2 tablespoons minced parsley

2 medium tomatoes, chopped

2 cloves garlic, minced

1 large onion, chopped

2 green peppers, seeded and cut in strips

2 medium zucchini, in 1/2" (10 mm) slices

1 small eggplant peeled and cut in 1" (25 mm) cubes

4 tablespoons canola or olive oil

1 medium potato, diced (optional)

Instructions

In a pressure cooker, heat half of the oil then stir fry the potato, zucchini and eggplant in small batches then place them onto a warm platter. Add in the rest of the oil and the garlic and onion then sauté until the onion is well browned and return the veggies and the other ingredients to the cooker. Cover the cooker and then bring it to maximum pressure by heating on high heat then lower the heat. Cook for 3 minutes on high pressure then allow the cooker to release pressure through the quick release method. Remove the lid and check the amount of stew; if it is too much, simmer while uncovered for a few minutes then serve.

Beef Stew

Makes 4 servings

Ingredients

Salt and pepper

2 bay leaves

1 ½ teaspoons thyme

1 tablespoon brown sugar

2 tablespoons balsamic vinegar

2 tablespoons tomato paste

1 (14 ounce) cans tomatoes, un-drained

½ cup chopped carrot

2 cups diced potatoes

2 tablespoons minced garlic

½ cup chopped onion

½ cup beef broth

1 ½ teaspoons olive oil

1 lb lean beef, cubed

¼ teaspoon dry mustard

½ teaspoon salt

¼ cup flour

Instructions

Mix salt, dry mustard and flour in a bag then add beef and shake to coat.

In the pressure cooker, heat the oil and brown pieces of beef before adding broth and bringing the contents to a boil. Add the other ingredients that are remaining.

Cover with the lid and heat the cooker to high heat to bring the cooker to maximum pressure then cook for about 12 minutes and then remove lid and discard the bay leaves before serving.

Mushroom Beef Stew

Makes 4 servings

Ingredients

1 -2 beef bouillon cubes (optional)

10-20 ounces water

10 ounces condensed golden mushroom soup

8 -12 rinsed and halved button mushrooms

1 -2 teaspoons dried parsley

Salt & pepper

4 red potatoes cut into chunks

4 carrots, peeled and cut into chunks

1 large onion, cut up

1 ½ lbs stew meat

2 tablespoons canola oil

Instructions

Place the oil in a pressure cooker then heat it until hot then add in the meat and cook unturned for a minute to allow it to sear then stir the meat to let it brown on all sides then add carrots, salt, onions, parsley, water, beef, potatoes, mushrooms, pepper and golden mushroom soup.

Lock the lid, and heat the cooker to high heat until the pressure is at its maximum. Cook for 15 minutes then cool the cooker immediately and then serve.

To make the stew thicker, stir 1 tablespoon cornstarch with ½ cup water and add to the stew, then boil the stew until it thickens.

Southern Red Beans & Rice stew

Makes 8 servings

Ingredients

7 cups water

1 lb dried red kidney beans, sorted

1 teaspoon liquid smoke

1 tablespoon Worcestershire sauce

2 bay leaves

1 teaspoon dried thyme

¼ teaspoon freshly ground pepper

½ teaspoon cayenne pepper

2 teaspoons kosher salt

3 tablespoons garlic, chopped

½ cup celery, chopped

1 bell pepper, chopped

1 ½ cups onions, chopped

3 tablespoons olive oil

Instructions

Heat olive oil in pressure cooker without the lid over medium heat then sauté the celery, garlic, bell pepper and the onions for 5 minutes and then add all the remaining ingredients.

Attach the lid to the pressure cooker then heat until the cooker attains maximum pressure, lower the heat and then cook for 45 minutes at high pressure. Allow the pressure to release naturally then remove the pot from the heat.

Remove the lid after the cooker has cooled and all the pressure has been released then use a slotted spoon to remove the bay leaves. You can smash the beans using the potato smasher, then stir for 5 minutes in low heat to allow the stew to thicken. If necessary, add water or adjust seasoning to add taste. You can serve the stew over hot cooked rice or garnish with hot sauce or green onion as desired.

Conclusion

I want to thank you so much for your purchase and your time. I hope that you can now add some variety to your daily meals with these pressure cooker recipes I have provided you. I know you and your family will just love them all!

The only real question left is which one will become your favorite?

If you are fan of great desserts then I would recommend that you take a sneak peek at one of my other popular recipe books called "DUMP CAKE - 50+ Top Dump Cake Recipes For Easy And Delicious Desserts". As a free bonus I have included a free preview for you on the next page.

Thank-you

Sara Banks

Free Preview "Dump Cake Recipes"

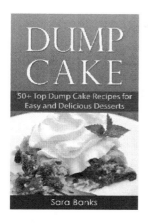

#15: Pumpkin filling dump cake

Ingredients

3 eggs

1 can pumpkin puree

½ cup of white sugar

½ cup of packed brown sugar

1 teaspoon of ground cinnamon

1 (12 ounce) can evaporated milk

¼ teaspoon of ground cloves

½ teaspoon of ground ginger

1 (18.25 oz) package of spice cake mix

½ teaspoon of salt

½ cup of melted butter

½ cup of coarsely chopped pecans

Directions

Preheat oven to 350 degrees F and then grease a 9x13 inch pan. Combine eggs, pumpkin puree, brown sugar, milk and white sugar in a large bowl. Stir in the ginger, cinnamon, salt and cloves, and transfer into the greased pan. Sprinkle in the dry cake mix, and top with pecans then add in melted butter, and bake in the preheated oven until lightly brown for about 55 minutes. Allow to cool and then serve warm.

#16: Yellow cake mix pineapple cake

Ingredients

1 can cherry pie filling

1 can crushed pineapple

¾ cup of melted butter

1 box of yellow cake mix

½ cup of chopped nuts

1 cup of chocolate chips

Directions

Pour the ingredients in a 9x12-inch pan and bake in a 350 degrees F preheated oven until done for about fifty minutes.

You can also transfer all the ingredients in a crock-pot and cook until set for about 2-3 hours.

#17: Apple pie filling milk dump cake

Ingredients

For the Cake:

3 eggs

1 box of yellow cake mix

1 can of apple pie filling

For frosting

2 sticks butter, softened

4 cups of powdered sugar

3 tablespoons of milk

Directions

For the Cake:

Beat 3 large eggs slightly in a bowl then sprinkle the cake mix over the eggs until it becomes thick dough. Mix in the pie filling with a wooden spoon and then grease and flour the cake pans or your baking dish. Blend using your hand mixer or stand mixer.

For Frosting:

Beat the butter in a bowl, add powdered sugar gently, and add a little milk if the mixture becomes too thick. Stir in the listed flavors below:

Apple pie filling: Stir in 3 teaspoons of cinnamon to the frosting.

Cherry pie filling: Stir in 1 tablespoon of almond extract.

Chocolate frosting: Stir in cocoa powder

#18: white vinegar vanilla cake

Ingredients

1 teaspoon of salt

3 cups of flour

6 tablespoons of cocoa

2 cups of sugar

2 tablespoons of white vinegar

¾ cup olive oil

2 teaspoons of vanilla

2 cups of cold water

2 teaspoons of baking soda

Directions

Preheat oven to 350 degrees F. Combine all the ingredients, and transfer into an ungreased pan then bake for 35 minutes in the preheated oven, or until the inserted toothpick at the center comes out clean.

#19: Caramel sauce dump cake

Ingredients

2 cans of apple pie filling, or blueberry or cherry

2 sticks of butter, melted

1 box of yellow cake mix

½ teaspoon of cinnamon (optional)

½ cup caramel sauce

Whipped cream for garnish (optional)

½ cup chopped pecans (optional)

Instructions

Combine caramel sauce and apple pie filling in a greased baking dish. Add 1/2 teaspoon of cinnamon, if you so desire, and spread evenly in the apple pie filling pan. Sprinkle in the dry cake mix and spread evenly then top with pecans and melted butter and bake for 45-50 minutes at 350 degrees F or until golden brown at the top and becomes bubbly at the edges.

Serve with whipped cream and ice cream.